# ORSON'S FARM™
## COUNTS ITS CHICKENS 2

### JIM DAVIS

ℛℛ
RAVETTE BOOKS

This edition first published by Ravette Books Limited 1988

Printed and bound in Great Britain
for Ravette Books Limited,
3 Glenside Estate, Star Road, Partridge Green,
Horsham, Sussex RH13 8RA
by Cox & Wyman Ltd, Reading

ISBN 1 85304 076 2

© 1987 United Feature Syndicate, Inc.

© 1987 United Feature Syndicate, Inc.

© 1987 United Feature Syndicate, Inc.

JIM DAVIS 1-30

© 1987 United Feature Syndicate, Inc.

JIM DAVIS 2·14

1987 United Feature Syndicate Inc

© 1987 United Feature Syndicate, Inc.

JIM DAVIS 2-27

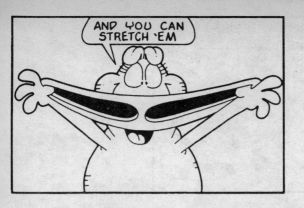

© 1987 United Feature Syndicate, Inc.

JIM DAVIS 3-22

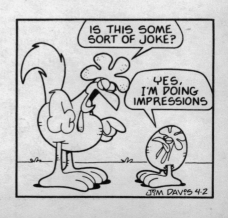

© 1987 United Feature Syndicate, Inc.   JIM DAVIS 4-6

CHONK

© 1987 United Feature Syndicate, Inc.

JIM DAVIS 4-13

# Other JIM DAVIS books published by Ravette

**In this series**

| | |
|---|---|
| Goes Half Hog! 1 | £1.95 |
| Goes Half Hog! 2 | £1.95 |
| Counts Its Chickens 1 | £1.95 |
| Rules The Roost 1 | £1.95 |
| Rules The Roost 2 | £1.95 |

**Garfield Pocket books**

| No. 1 | Garfield The Great Lover | £1.95 |
|---|---|---|
| No. 2 | Garfield Why Do You Hate Mondays? | £1.95 |
| No. 3 | Garfield Does Pooky Need You? | £1.95 |
| No. 4 | Garfield Admit It, Odie's OK! | £1.95 |
| No. 5 | Garfield Two's Company | £1.95 |
| No. 6 | Garfield What's Cooking? | £1.95 |
| No. 7 | Garfield Who's Talking? | £1.95 |
| No. 8 | Garfield Strikes Again | £1.95 |
| No. 9 | Garfield Here's Looking At You | £1.95 |
| No. 10 | Garfield We Love You Too | £1.95 |
| No. 11 | Garfield Here We Go Again | £1.95 |
| No. 12 | Garfield Life and Lasagne | £1.95 |
| No. 13 | Garfield In The Pink | £1.95 |
| No. 14 | Garfield Just Good Friends | £1.95 |
| No. 15 | Garfield Plays It Again | £1.95 |
| No. 16 | Garfield Flying High | £1.95 |

All these books are available at your local bookshop or news-agent, or can be ordered direct from the publisher. Just tick the titles you require and fill in the form below. Prices and availability subject to change without notice. A full list of our publications is available. Please send your request to the address below.

**Ravette Books Limited, 3 Glenside Estate, Star Road, Partridge Green, Horsham, West Sussex RH13 8RA**

Please send a cheque or postal order, and allow the following for postage and packing. UK: 45p for one book plus 20p for the second book and 15p for each additional book.

Name ...............................................................................................

Address ...............................................................................................

...............................................................................................